HOW DO YOU SURVIVE WHEN MUM & DAD SEPARATE

A book written by a girl like you

Copyright © 2021 by Caroline Martins

All rights reserved. No part of this book may be reproduced, distributed, or transmitted in any form or by any means, including photocopying, recording, or other electronic or mechanical methods, except in the case of brief quotations embodied in critical reviews, without the prior written permission of the author.

ISBN 9798773821175

The strategies in this book are presented for educational purposes. All quotes remain the proprietary property of the authors. Every effort has been made to trace copyright holders and obtain permission for the use of copyrights material where applicable.

The information and resources presented are based on the author's personal experience and opinion. Any outcome or results vary with each individual. There is no guarantee as to the results.

The author reserves all rights to make changes and assumes no responsibility or liability on behalf of any purchaser, reader or user of these materials.

First Edition

ACKNOWLEDGEMENTS

Where do I even start?

Many people helped me get to where I am today!

I would first like to thank my amazing and "trés attentionnée" grandma, Edite, for helping me go through the separation followed by many hugs and kisses. Je t'aime beaucoup, un grand bisou!

I would like to thank Beren, my caring and marvellous bonus-dad, for all your love and help in giving me a boost of happiness when I was down. I am very grateful for our dad and daughter talks to ensure that I was good and had a happy mindset at the end. Ik houd van je!

My dear sister, Catherine, how could I not thank you! You are a fantastic sister. I'm very lucky to have you. I'm very happy to have had your help in correcting my many drafts and ensuring that every little detail was good. Thank you for making time especially due to all the exams you have been having to help me and giving me superb ideas.
I love ya!

Lastly, I would like to thank my wonderful "Wonder Woman Mum", Eva Martins for all your support and guidance during this journey. Without you this book wouldn't be out exploring the world. I'm very grateful for your help and advice to make this book awesome. Even with your busy schedule and work I am very happy that you made time to help me. Your small and sometimes long talks have helped me so much in becoming a better and happier girl.
I love you very much!

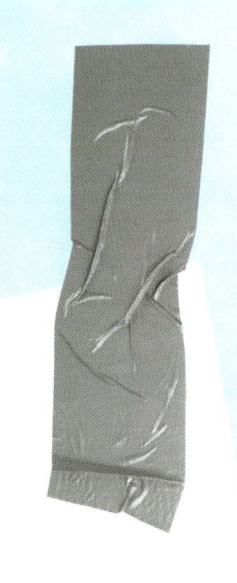

I wrote this book to help you go through divorce, meanwhile also helping myself to let go of my fears and struggles. It was an exhausting process of going through it myself. I suffered a lot. I would love to help you navigate this period without feeling alone. Remembering it is not your fault even when you think otherwise. I understand you. I have been there. But we will get through this together!

PART 1

1 – Who am I?
2 – Why did I write this book?
3 – What is a divorce?
4 – Before the divorce
5 – During the divorce
6 – How I felt after the divorce
7 – IT'S FUN ACTIVITY TIME!
8 – Going through separation
9 – How to get through separation

PART 2

1 – Moving homes
2 – How I felt when I moved to Switzerland
3 – Let's do some fun activities
4 – How did I get new friends
5 – How can you do the same
6 – The 5 key takeaways!
7 – How to connect with me

I wake up from my beautiful dream, sometimes a nightmare. I put my clothes on and brush my hair. I go downstairs and have my delicious yoghurt with fruit. Thinking to myself if I had finished my homework. I put my spoon in the dishwasher, and the plastic can in the garbage. I go upstairs and brush my teeth. I feed my turtles dried small shrimps. The shrimps are tinier than my thumb, and they look light brown, like the color of the sand. The turtles are tinier than my tiny hand. They are green, and their shell looks like the color of dirty grass, with a lot of lines on it. The water is the color of a sunny day at the beach. I looked at them and they stared at me, as if they were saying, can you get out? We want to eat!

WHO AM I?

> My name is Caroline, I'm 12 years old. I was born in Portugal, and am half French. I can see where I get my love for bread! :) I moved to Switzerland when I was 6 years old, sometime after my parents divorce. My dad is Portuguese and my mum is French. I have a sister who is 16 years old, a bonus brother who's 6, and another bonus brother who's 13 years old, and a bonus dad and a bonus mum. My bonus brother, who is 13 years old, lives in Switzerland with me, and my bonus brother, who is 6, lives with my dad and bonus mum. Happy big families! My favorite food is sushi and cucumbers, and I love fruit and vegetables. I enjoy volleyball, running, reading, drawing, baking, ballet and modern dance. At school I did cross country, it was very fun and accomplished many goals. I still run sometimes with my sister. I am also very grateful for being able to dance in a professional dance school. Now that you have learned quite a bit about me it is my turn to learn a bit about you too!

WHO ARE YOU?

_____

_____

_____

_____

_____

_____

_____

_____

_____

_____

_____

_____

_____

WHO ARE YOU?
_____

WHAT MAKES YOU, YOU?

_____

_____

_____

_____

_____

_____

_____

_____

_____

_____

_____

_____

_____

WHAT MAKES YOU, YOU?

WHAT IS AFFECTING OR WORRYING YOU?

_____

_____

_____

_____

_____

_____

_____

_____

_____

_____

_____

_____

_____

WHAT ARE YOU AFRAID OF IN THIS JOURNEY?

WHAT ARE YOU GOING TO DO TO FEEL AMAZING?

_____

_____

_____

_____

_____

_____

_____

_____

_____

_____

_____

_____

> "I think it is time to dig into the next pages, don't you think?"

WHY DID I WRITE THIS BOOK?

> "I wrote this book because I want to help you go through separation, moving and making friends in an easier way and not feel alone through this journey. I also want you to be happy. My goal by the end of the book is for us to be able to let go of the past and move forward as more adventures are waiting for you. Even though I'm 12 I have experienced this and I'm glad to be making this book for you."

WHAT IS DIVORCE?

Divorce is when 2 parents don't love each other anymore and they decide to separate. This means that they are no longer together nor married anymore.

MUM ← → DAD

BEFORE THE DIVORCE

> It was a sunny day. I was playing football with my dad, dog and sister. Well, my dog was running around trying to get the ball. While my mum was cooking. It smelled like home cooked lasagna, so good I told myself. My dad kicked the ball at me, but I couldn't reach it. It fell inside the cold, blue pool. I heard a loud splash. Why did it have to fall inside the cold pool, I asked myself. That gave me shivers. But then my mum called me to have lunch and I didn't mind anymore about the ball, instead I could feel the warm lasagna coming towards me. When I entered the kitchen, I saw that it was white fish and salad. Why white fish!!!! Why!! I said in my head. I don't like white fish!!!!

HOW I FELT WHEN DURING THE DIVORCE

> When my parents separated, I felt heartbroken, I was so sad. The worst part was that I thought it was my fault, when it wasn't. I always cried at night, and I couldn't fall asleep. Just the picture in my head of them fighting always made me cry. I never wanted to admit that they weren't getting back together. I always thought there would be a chance, but after some time of talking to my counselor, I learned that it was for the best. That it was a good choice they made, otherwise they would always be fighting constantly and feel unhappy. So, I just told myself that it was for the best and the universe did it for a reason. Sometimes I still cry, but who wouldn't? We have to get it all out. Now I feel much better, I'm happy and I have 2 families that love me very much. Do you know the good thing about having two families? It's that then you will get double the presents and double the love, and of course much more. Haha!!! 😊
>
> When my mum found a boyfriend, I didn't really like it because I thought that he was going to take my dad's place but that's not true and I realized that when I spent more time with him and I talked to my mum, now he is married to my mum and I'm really happy about that. If one of your parent's makes you feel like that, just talk to them, ok? Even though I didn't have the courage before to talk to him it doesn't mean that you will also not be courageous like me. I know that you can do it. You are brave and don't worry because talking to him will make you feel much better.

AFTER THE DIVORCE

> "I could hear my parents from downstairs screaming at each other, and my sister and I were wondering what was going on. Their screaming felt like my ears were going to pop off. Luckily, they didn't!"

POP!

GOING THROUGH SEPARATION

> When your parents divorce it feels like the inside of you is all black, and you can't feel anything, you are frozen right? If you didn't feel that then that's ok, if you did, I felt the same way. So that's also ok to be like that. The most important thing is that you have to know that it's not your fault! Ok. what happens is that your parents will have a lot of stupid fights about stupid things because they're starting to not love each other anymore, and to hide their feelings they fight about stupid things. In the end they will make the choice to separate, so that they don't fight anymore, and so that their kids (which is you) can have a healthy life, without them worrying about their parents. I know it's sad but it's for the best.
>
> When my parents separated, I decided to always write my emotions down in a diary, so that it can all get out of my head. I also spoke to the counselor of my school (as you might already know) because then it would be less embarrassing, and so that she could help me feel better. It really helped. After a few months I decided to open up and talk to my mum because I wanted her to know what was going on. I was really nervous, but at the end I really didn't have to be. My mum helped me so much and I felt so much better. You don't have to be afraid to talk to your parents, they will never get mad at you. The only thing they will do is help you through every step of the way, like my mum did with me.

WHATEVER HAPPENS YOUR PARENTS WILL ALWAYS LOVE YOU!

IT'S FUN ACTIVITY TIME!

1 - COLOR US!

There will be ups

...and downs

but you will get through them

and become stronger!

2 - WHAT ARE 5 THINGS THAT HAPPENED TODAY THAT MADE YOU HAPPY:

1

2

3

4

5

3 - WHAT ARE 5 THINGS THAT YOU WOULD LIKE TO HAVE OR DO:

1

2

3

4

5

> Perfect, now we can go onto the next important topic in separation ...

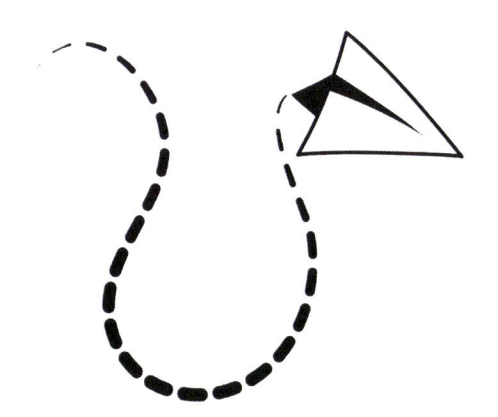

HOW TO GET THROUGH SEPARATION

You probably have a lot of questions circulating your head right now and are unsure of the right answer. Well there is no right answer but there are exercises and activities you can do to feel better, which I will be uncovering today.

Going through separation is hard, I know, but that's why I'm here. If you would like you can do what I am going to tell you or you can do something else, everything is good. If you would like, you could have a diary, one that is blank, and write 5 things that you are grateful for everyday and 5 things that you would like to achieve or get better at. That is what I used to do, and don't worry if you forget sometimes just try to remember to do it because it helps release clustered emotions. You can also write about your day, how it was, what you did and if you would like what went well and what didn't go so well.

In addition, you can also have a diary which you and your mum/dad write in so you can send each other messages or if something exciting happened, anything that you would like.

It's also good because if you don't want to say something you can just write it down. Also remember to be positive and smile as much as you can, it makes you feel better. If you would like, you could also ask your mum/dad if one day you could have a mother/father and daughter/son time. Just have a lot of fun together and connect. There are many other things you could do but these are the ones that worked the best for me.

I have listed the ones that have helped me the most but now listen to your amazing head and think about the ones that helped or could help you to go through separation by answering these two quick questions…

What are some exercises you would like to try doing?

1.

2.

3.

What other exercises you think could help you (not listed above)?

1.

2.

3.

PART 2

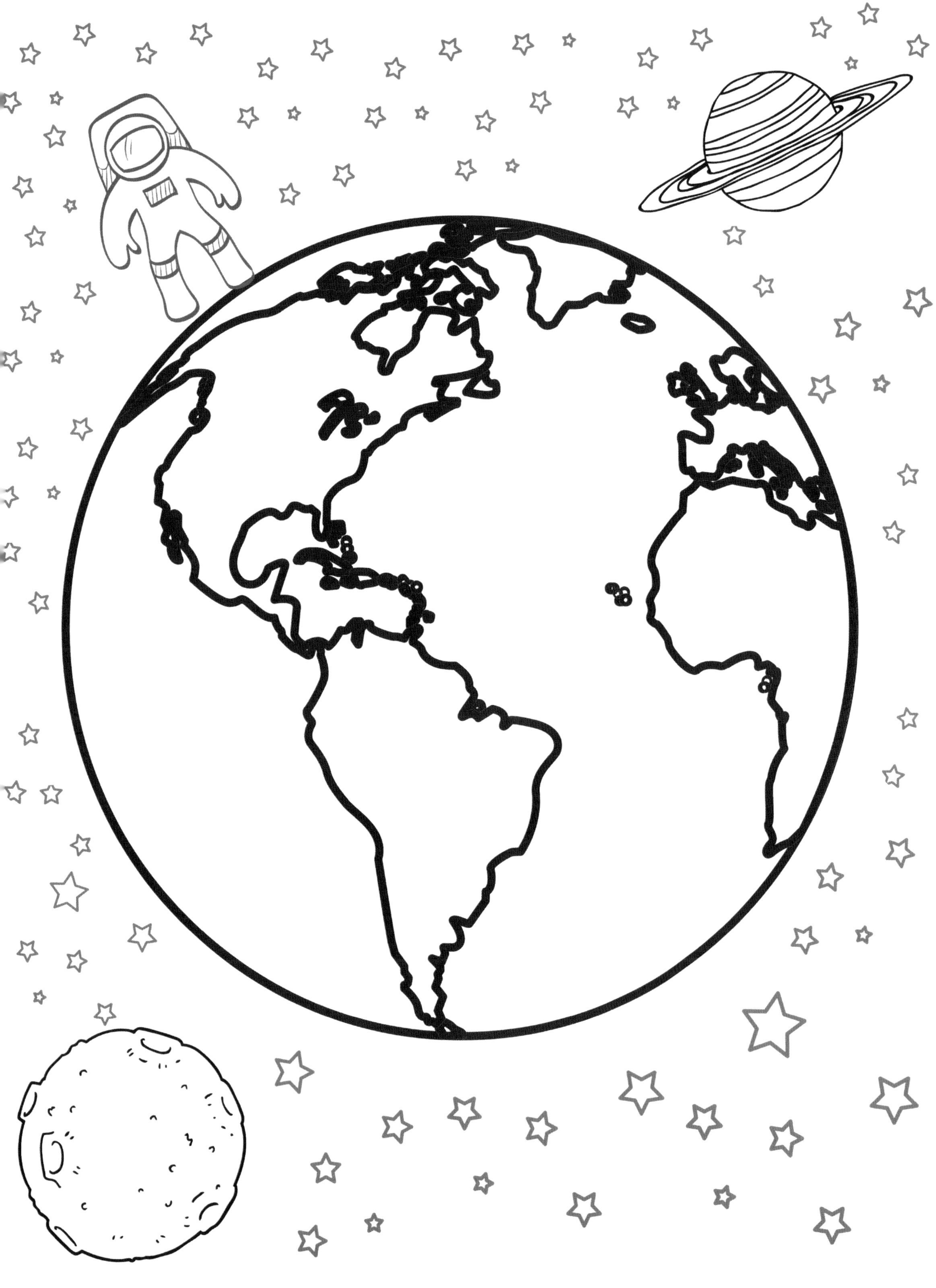

> Now it's "moving" time, how to make friends and how to feel comfortable at your new school

MOVING

It's an uncomfortable word to hear... it feels like you are letting go a part of your identity. When you move to a new country or a new city or anywhere, it's different right? It feels a bit weird, don't you think? It's a different place than the one you were used to, one you don't know much about. But, it can also be exciting because you get to see and do new things.

It might be different because you don't know the language but the cool thing about it is that you can learn it and then you'll know a new language. You might miss your other place, but you can always ask your parents to go visit it every once in a while. And you have two homes now.

HOW I FELT WHEN I MOVED TO SWITZERLAND

> When I moved to Switzerland, I barely knew how to speak English and didn't even know German existed. It was a completely new place to me and a different schedule to adapt to. Especially the snow, in Portugal or at least Lisbon it doesn't snow so it was really cool to be able to touch and see it. I miss Lisbon of course but now I live in Switzerland, and I really like it here too. I still visit Portugal because my dad lives there, and I miss him too. I have awesome friends, an awesome family and of course a lovely and crazy cat, and 2 turtles. In Portugal I also have an awesome family and two lovely and crazy dogs. When I moved I was upset because I missed my dad a lot and I wanted my mum and dad to be together but my mum said that the universe does things for a purpose and I didn't like when she kept on saying that but then she said that it's my choice though to decide how I wanna go through it and what I want to feel, after some time I realized that that was awesome advice and I decided to choose to go through it in a positive way. So, it's your choice to decide how you want to feel and how you want to go through it. You can be lazy and do nothing and keep on crying which is also ok, or you can get up and be positive and happy, you can still cry but at least you are forcing yourself to get up and be positive which brings you to a better place at the end and that is what you call being strong and getting the negative energy out of your way and making it positive. That is very admirable to some people because some people are too scared to do that which is also ok but if you get up you become an example of strength and bravery.

LET'S DO ANOTHER FUN ACTIVITY

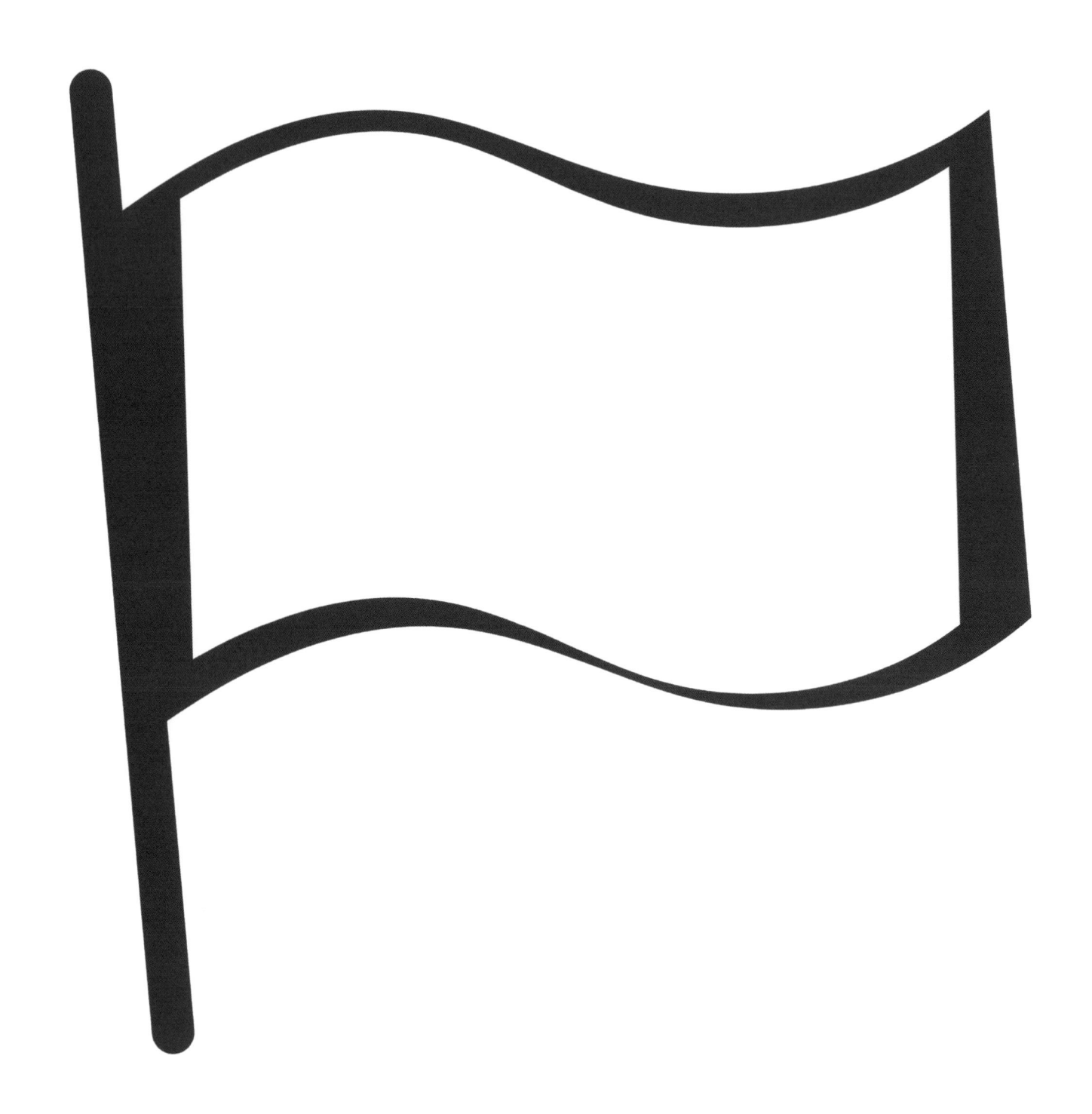

Draw your flag in here

...and your family in here

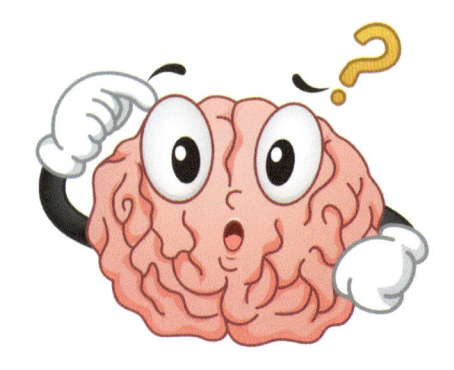

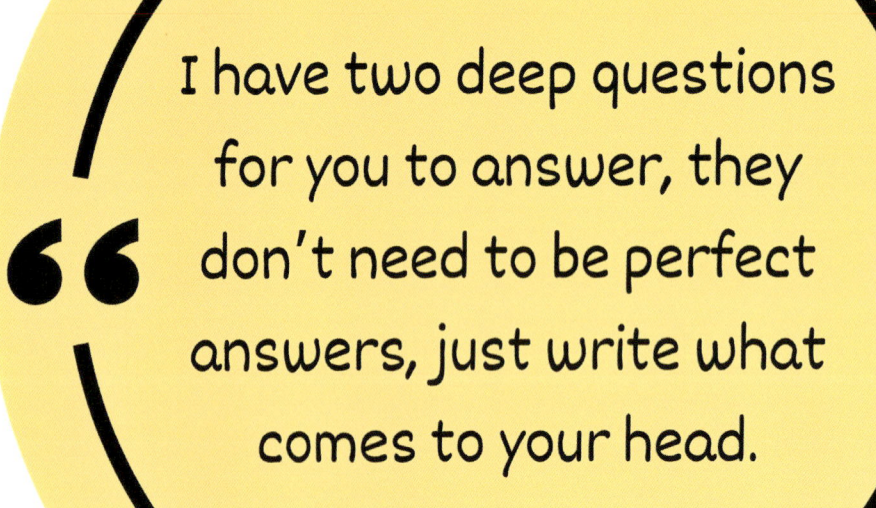

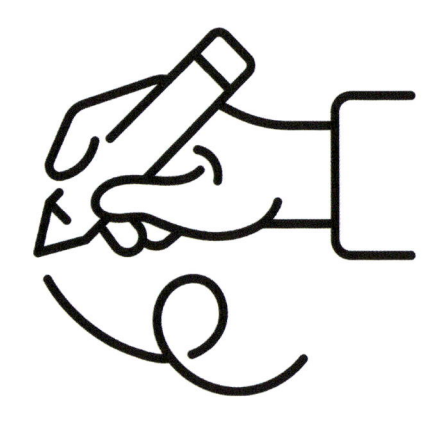

"I have two deep questions for you to answer, they don't need to be perfect answers, just write what comes to your head."

1. WHAT DO YOU LOVE ABOUT YOUR PARENTS?

_____
_____
_____
_____
_____
_____
_____
_____
_____
_____
_____

2. IF YOU CHANGED LOCATION, WHAT ARE SOME THINGS YOU LIKE ABOUT THAT AREA?

_____

_____

_____

_____

_____

_____

_____

_____

_____

_____

_____

HOW I GOT FRIENDS

> The most important thing is being yourself if you want to get friends because you are showing that you accept yourself and that you love yourself. I started talking to the people that I thought would be nice to have as friends, even though I didn't really know English I tried to communicate with them. I made really nice friends. On my second year in Basel I was much better in English. I tried speaking as much as I could to my friends in English and it paid off a lot. In my second year I found a new girl and she knew English much better than I did. She was quiet and very nice. I talked to her and she talked to me, after some time we were not as quiet as some people thought we were. We were crazy and funny when it was just the two of us. We still are. Now I have more friends, some of them moved but my best friends are still here with me. We all are super crazy and loud, but when we are inside, we are pretty quiet. We all are awesome friends and don't forget about crazy. I know that you will make friends easier than it looks like. Just be yourself. That's the most important.

MAKING FRIENDS

When making friends it is important to be yourself! But to make friends you have to communicate with people. For some of you, getting out of your comfort zone can be challenging, as you might not like talking with people you don't really know. I had the same problem; I was a very shy person until my friends pushed me out of my comfort zone for the better. I can still be very shy, but I have definitely improved and so can you. You just have to ask yourself how bad you want a friend, and if you really want one then you can get one. Everyone wants a friend! I love my friends. They are so awesome and friendly. One thing to remember is that quantity doesn't matter but the quality does. This means that you don't have to have many friends but good ones. When I came to ISB I have to admit I wanted lots of friends, and unfortunately that was what destroyed some of my friendships. I wasn't really thinking about who I had but that I wanted more. After some time, I realised that it wasn't about the quantity but the quality. My mum played a big role in helping me with my friendships. She is the one that helped me have the friends I have today! I know you will make amazing friends! Remember to also listen to your friends as then they will not only open up more to you, but they will respect you and listen to you. It creates a much stronger bond between you two. Depending on the people it may take longer to make friends, and that is perfectly fine. Everyone is different and that is what makes every single person unique and exciting to meet. Last advice, sometimes you might compare yourself/ your story to your friends or other people. I did too, but remember; we each have our own journey, obstacles and adventures. Your story is yours and only yours, and that is what makes you special, exciting and unique.

Whatever happens, never stop being you. You are a gift to the world!

> We have a couple more things to see so onto the next adventure of this book! I'll see you on the next page!

"It has come!
Can I get a drum roll please! ...."

THE TOP FIVE TAKEAWAYS FROM THIS BOOK!

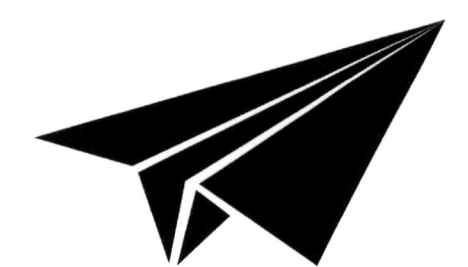

> "You might be thinking more reading noooo! But it will be fun, and very worth it!"

❶

Be open minded to new possibilities as you don't know what is waiting for you!

❷

The universe does things for a reason! I know you might think that is not true as you have had bad moments, but you learn new things from those experiences. Look how far you've come!

3

Don't compare yourself to other people as you are completely different and special in your own way. This is your road not the other persons.

4

Be yourself! You go much further in life when you are being yourself.

5

It is ok to ask for help and show your emotions! Everyone has cried and asked for help or shown different emotions. No one is perfect!

HOW DO I FEEL?

HOW HAVE I CHANGED?

> The last exercise I would like you to do is to ask yourself…

AND… HOW HAVE I GROWN THROUGH THIS JOURNEY?

> **YOU ARE AMAZING, STRONG AND COURAGEOUS, DON'T EVER FORGET THAT!**

If you ever wish to talk to me in private then contact me through this email right here:
carolinemartins.mumanddad@gmail.com

Printed in Great Britain
by Amazon